MONTY PANESAR

UNAUTHORISED BIOGRAPHY

Claire Throp

Raintree

www.raintreepublishers.co.uk
Visit our website to find out more information about Raintree books.

To order:
☎ Phone 44 (0) 1865 888112
▤ Send a fax to 44 (0) 1865 314091
▦ Visit the Raintree bookshop at www.raintreepublishers.co.uk to browse our catalogue and order online.

Raintree is an imprint of Pearson Education Limited, a company incorporated in England and Wales having its registered office at Edinburgh Gate, Harlow, Essex, CM20 2JE – Registered company number: 00872828

Raintree is a registered trademark of Pearson Education Limited

Editorial: Catherine Veitch
Design: Richard Parker and Q2A Solutions
Illustrations: Oxford Designers and Illustrators
Picture research: Mica Brancic
Production: Victoria Fitzgerald
Originated by DOT Gradations Ltd
Printed and bound in China by CTPS

ISBN 978 1 4062 0952 5
12 11 10 09 08
10 9 8 7 6 5 4 3 2 1

British Library Cataloguing in Publication Data
Throp, Claire
Monty Panesar. — (Sport files)
796.7'2'092
A full catalogue record for this book is available from the British Library.

Acknowledgements
We would like to thank the following for permission to reproduce photographs: © Action Images pp. **5** (Jason O'Brien Livepic), **16** (Tim Wimborne), **26** (Alex Morton); © Corbis/Reuters/Luke MacGregor p. **9**; © Getty Images pp. **7** (888.com), **15** (Clive Rose), **21** (Stu Forster), **25** (ECB), **27** (Dave M. Benett); © Hamish Blair/Getty Images p. **18**; © PA Photos/EMPICS Sport/Paul Marriott p. **10**; © Philip Brown p. **11**; © Reuters pp. **13** (Adnan Abidi), **19** (Corbis/David Gray), **23** (Stephen Hird).

Cover photograph of Monty Panesar appealing to the umpire for a wicket at the Third Test match between England and India at the Oval in August 2007, reproduced with permission of ©Getty Images/ Hamish Blair.

Every effort has been made to contact copyright holders of material reproduced in this book. Any omissions will be rectified in subsequent printings if notice is given to the publishers.

Contents

A new star... 4

Early years 6

School and cricket 8

First class career 10

A dream come true... 12

Five-wicket haul... 14

Monty comes of age 16

The Ashes tour 2006–07.. 18

Ups and downs... 20

Monty's star shines 22

An epic battle 24

"The Monty effect" 26

Timeline 28

Amazing facts.. 29

Glossary 30

Find out more 31

Index.. 32

Some words are shown in bold, **like this.** You can find out what they mean by looking in the glossary.

It is difficult to believe that Monty Panesar has only been in the public eye since March 2006. His cricketing achievements in that short amount of time have been huge. By the end of 2007, Monty had taken 92 international test **wickets** and 24 **one-day** international wickets. He's taken five wickets in a match seven times, a ten-wicket haul once, and was the highest-placed bowler for England in the test rankings in summer 2007. Add to that how well he's done for his club, Northamptonshire, and it is clear that Monty is a talented bowler.

FAST FACT FILE

Name:	Mudhsuden Singh Panesar
Nickname:	Monty
Born:	25 April 1982, Luton, Bedfordshire
Family:	Mum Gursharan, dad Paramjit, brother Isher, sister Charanjit
Height:	6 ft 1 in
Batting style:	Left-hand bat
Bowling style:	Left-arm spin
Best International Bowling:	6 wickets for 126 runs against New Zealand, March 2008
Teams:	England, British Universities, Loughborough University, Northamptonshire, Bedfordshire, Luton Town and Indians Cricket Club
Rankings:	June 2007 gained a best of 721, which gave him 6th place in the ICC test rankings (see box on page 22).

Exciting spin

Spin bowlers are normally thought of as less interesting than **fast bowlers**, probably because the ball is bowled at a slower pace. But Monty has followed in the footsteps of Australia's Shane Warne and Muttiah Muralitharan of Sri Lanka and shown the world that spinners can be just as exciting to watch as fast bowlers.

Monty has become famous for his enthusiastic galloping celebrations when he has taken a wicket. His obvious love of the game is part of the reason why he has become a crowd favourite. "Monty mania" has inspired many spectators to come to cricket matches dressed up as their hero. His club, Northamptonshire, even provided a special area for fans to sit together during the **Twenty20** games in 2007. Monty has gained a strong following very quickly.

All cricketers like to celebrate when they have got a player out, but Monty celebrates more than most!

Mudhsuden Singh Panesar, also known as Monty, was born in Luton on 25 April 1982. Monty's parents had come to England from India in the 1970s. A few years after they arrived Monty was born. Later they had another son, Isher, and then a daughter, Charanjit.

When he was four years old, Monty visited India for the first time. He didn't really enjoy the trip as he didn't like the large number of flies or the cows that wandered down the middle of the street! It was where his parents were born, though, so there were many more family holidays there for him to get used to it.

SIKHISM

Monty's family are **Sikhs**. They follow the religion of Sikhism. Sikhism began in a northern area of India called the Punjab. Sikhs worship one god. They do not gamble or drink alcohol, and they give to charity as often as they can. Monty has never eaten meat or cut his hair – both these things are part of the rules of Sikhism. He can speak English and the Indian language, Punjabi, equally well.

Mudhsuden or Monty?

Monty's real name, Mudhsuden, comes from Madhusudanah, which is one of the names of a Sikh god called Krishna. It was one of Monty's aunts who gave him the nickname "Monty" when he was young. It was only later, when he began to play at cricket clubs, that the nickname really stuck. The other players sometimes found his real name – Mudhsuden – difficult to say.

Monty's favourite snooker player was Jimmy White, mainly because he was left-handed, the same as Monty!

A new cricket fan

Monty played many sports when he was young, including tennis, snooker, and football. Monty was nine years old before he decided to try cricket. His first club was Luton Town and Indians Cricket Club. His coach was a friend of the family, Hitu Naik. Monty took part in the Sunday morning cricket sessions and from then on couldn't stop thinking about cricket, both playing it himself and watching on television.

School and cricket

Monty started off as a **medium pace bowler**, but in the winter of 1994 he was encouraged to change to spin bowling. Monty had big hands, even at the age of 12, and this helped him to spin the ball. Monty finally made the change to spin bowling in an Under-15s match. He got 7 **wickets** for only 35 **runs**.

Which school?

At the age of 16, Monty had to decide where to take his A-levels. Friends from school were going to one school, but his friends from the cricket team were going to Bedford Modern. This was because the school was well known for having good cricket **facilities**. Unfortunately, **fees** had to be paid to go to this school, so Monty wrote to them and told them that he planned to play cricket for a living. Luckily, the school offered him a sports **scholarship** so that his parents would not need to pay the fees.

At Bedford Modern, Monty gained three A-levels in chemistry, physics, and maths. At the same time, he was involved in achieving a new school record of winning 13 cricket matches in one year.

THE AIM OF CRICKET

There are eleven players in a cricket team. The person who is batting aims to score as many runs as possible. The bowler tries to get the person who is batting out. When the person who is batting is out, the bowler is said to have taken his or her wicket.

Monty bowls spin bowling, which is a slow form of bowling. A spinner tries to turn the ball as he or she bowls. Spinners have to work hard to get wickets by changing the pace and flight of the ball, in order to confuse the person who is batting.

Monty's hands measure nearly 28 cm (11 in) from his wrist to the top of his middle finger. His hands are so large that he can hold three cricket balls in his open hand.

University

In late summer 2001, Monty faced another big decision. He could either play cricket in another country over the winter, or he could go to university. Monty's county club, Northamptonshire, encouraged him to choose university. This was because he had a place at Loughborough University, the home of the Loughborough Cricket Centre of Excellence. This would allow Monty to study, at the same time as improving his cricket skills.

Monty was nervous about coping by himself, away from home, but he soon settled. He joined various clubs, including the Indian Society. One of the highlights of university for Monty was making the British Universities team. It meant that he could mix with players from universities all around the country and that he got to play against touring international teams, including Sri Lanka.

Monty joined Northamptonshire Cricket Club (see map on page 17) in 1998 as a professional cricketer. This meant he was able to earn money for playing cricket. In England, **first-class county cricket** is played by county teams like Northamptonshire and Lancashire. There are two divisions in first-class county cricket. At first, Monty played for the second team. In 2000, he was given the chance to play for the England under-19s against Sri Lanka.

Struggling for a place

His studies meant that he had only a couple of chances to appear for Northamptonshire during 2001. He did make his first-class **debut** against Leicestershire, though. It was an excellent start, as he took 8 **wickets** for just 131 **runs**. That year Monty won the Denis Compton award for Most Promising Young Player. The award is given to one player from each of the 18 first-class county teams at the end of a season. Although he was doing well, Monty did not find it easy to keep his place in the first team. Northamptonshire already had two spinners in Graeme Swann and Jason Brown.

Monty is seen here in his early playing days with Northamptonshire County Cricket Club.

Monty's coach at Northamptonshire, Kepler Wessels, suggested Monty should be picked for England's tour of India at the beginning of 2006.

Coaches

Monty was given the chance to go to the National Academy in Australia (see map on page 12) over the winter of 2002–03. In Australia he worked with former Australian cricketer, Rod Marsh, to try to improve his batting and **fielding** skills.

When Monty returned to Northamptonshire for the 2003 season, Kepler Wessels was the new team coach. Monty believes that Marsh and Wessels had a big influence on his cricket. "They don't praise you often and so when they said 'Well done!' it was like, 'Yeah!' ... With them you want to do well because you want to get a positive comment out of them."

A great year

In 2005 Graeme Swann left Northamptonshire and Monty finished university. This meant he was able to play in the first team, which had not been doing well. Monty helped them win some matches and to finish in fourth place in the second division.

In the winter of 2005, Monty travelled to Darren Lehmann's Academy in Adelaide, Australia to work on improving his poor batting and **fielding**. Monty had asked the England and Wales Cricket Board (ECB) for help. He knew that if he was to gain a place in the England team, he had to improve his all-round game.

Test debut

At the end of 2005 England's first choice spinner, Ashley Giles, was injured so Monty was picked for the test squad to tour India. **Test matches** are played over five days, with each team having two **innings**. An innings is when one team tries to score as many runs as they can, while the other team tries to bowl them out.

Monty's test **debut** took place at Nagpur on 1 March 2006. Despite his nerves, Monty took his first international **wicket** in India's first innings. It was his childhood hero Sachin Tendulkar. Monty's wild, galloping celebration, jumping for joy and throwing high fives at his teammates is now famous.

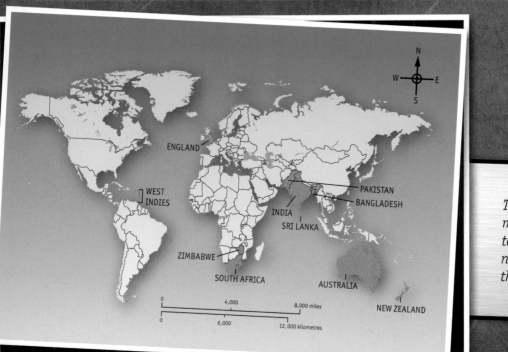

This world map shows the test-playing nations of the world.

Not all good

Monty went on to take two more wickers in the match. However, it was the contrast between Monty's skilful, attacking bowling and his almost comical fielding that attracted most attention.

Tendulkar actually signed the ball that got him out and gave it to Monty after the match.

There are many milestones (important events) in a cricketer's career. Obviously, the first milestone for any player is to be chosen for a first-class game. A player's first international **test match** is even more important.

Milestones in a bowler's career

For a bowler, it is then a case of how many **wickets** they can take in their career. The first wicket at each stage of cricket is the first event to celebrate. A five-wicket haul is when a bowler takes five wickets in an **innings**. A ten-wicket haul usually means that ten wickets are taken over a whole match rather than a single innings. Ten wickets are rarely taken in an innings, but it does happen occasionally.

It was during the third test against Sri Lanka at Trent Bridge (see map on page 17) in June 2006 that Monty achieved another bowling first: his first international five-wicket haul. While batting, Monty also surprised everyone by hitting the great **spin bowler**, Muttiah Muralitharan, for the maximum six **runs** in a single shot. It showed that his batting had definitely improved! Unfortunately, England still lost the match.

SIKH ROLE MODEL

Monty is the first **Sikh** to play cricket for England. In fact, he is the first Sikh to play for any country other than India. While he says this is not something he thinks about a lot, it makes him a **role model** for young Sikhs throughout the country. He points out that he is not the first Asian to play for the England team. But he is the first to wear a **patka**. A patka is a piece of cloth worn as a headcovering by Sikh males. "I'm proud of being the first Sikh to play for England, but my focus is on the cricket and that's what I'm there for," he says.

Left out

Monty had not been picked to play for England in the **one-day** series against Sri Lanka. Instead he returned to Northamptonshire and played in the **Twenty20** competition.

It was at this time that serious questions were being asked about Monty's **fielding**. It was sometimes so bad that a former England player, Michael Atherton, said he wasn't sure that Monty should be in the squad to tour Australia at the end of the year.

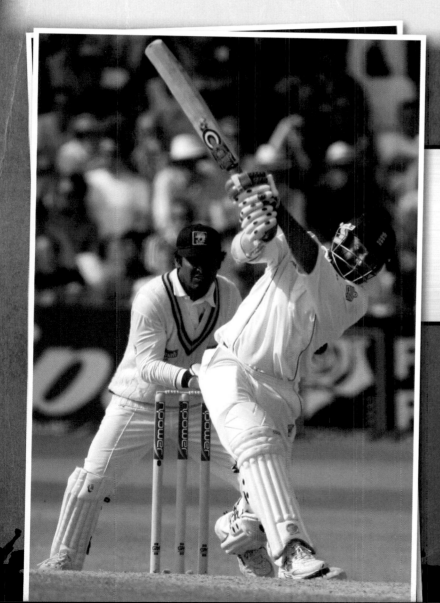

Monty bats at number 11, which means he bats last on his team – batting is not his strongpoint!

It was during Pakistan's tour of England in the summer of 2006 that Monty really came of age. Ashley Giles was still injured and Monty had a chance to play in the team. He took the opportunity with both of his huge hands!

Pakistan are known as a team who are able to handle spin bowling well. So Monty was extremely pleased with his success in the series. At Old Trafford in the second test, Monty took eight **wickets**, including five of the top six Pakistan batsmen in the second **innings**.

The third test

In the third test at Headingley (see map opposite), Monty took the wicket of Younis Khan. Monty believes it was his best ball for England so far. Younis Khan is very good at playing spin and was also playing really well at the time. The wicket was a brilliant one for Monty to get and Younis himself said "Well bowled" to Monty after the match.

Headingley was the start of the real hero worship of Monty by the crowds. People began to come to the matches wearing Monty masks, fake beards, and **patkas** in order to look like Monty. His fans didn't even seem to mind that his **fielding** wasn't very good. Every time he picked up the ball he got a cheer from the crowd.

Some people will go to extremes to look like their favourite player!

This map shows the seven test grounds in England. It also includes the ground of Monty's county club, Northamptonshire.

A break from cricket

Monty chose to take a complete break from cricket at the end of the 2006 season. He spent time with friends and even travelled to Canada to visit friends there.

Monty was not chosen to play in the International Cricket Council (ICC) Champions Trophy in September. However, later in the year he was picked for the **Ashes** tour in Australia and given a 12-month central contract with the England and Wales Cricket Board. This contract meant that Monty was likely to play a large part in the following year's international cricket.

The series of **test matches** that occurs between England and Australia every two years is known as the **Ashes**.

This is because in 1882, Australia beat England for the first time. In England there were newspaper stories claiming that this was the end of English cricket and that its ashes would be taken to Australia. England beat Australia the next time they played so a group of women burnt a wooden bail (part of the **wicket**) and put the ashes in a little urn.

Spinner Ashley Giles had been unable to play because of injury for some time before the first test. Nevertheless, he was chosen to play ahead of Monty. This was a surprise to most people, including the Australian team. They had talked about how they planned to make sure that Monty didn't have a chance to settle. This showed that they respected him and realised he was going to be a threat.

Finally!

In the third test, Monty finally got to play. England had already lost the first two games and had to win this game to save the series. Monty played well and managed to take eight wickets in all. Unfortunately, it wasn't enough and England lost the game.

Ashley Giles is congratulated by teammates after bowling out Ricky Ponting of Australia.

The supporters

Monty very quickly became a crowd favourite. However, there were some nasty comments from a few spectators. The situation didn't worry him though: "Maybe I don't get offended easily, but ... I want nothing to get in the way of my performance, so just laugh off anything from the crowd."

At New Year, Monty was invited by England captain, Andrew Flintoff, to watch the traditional fireworks from a boat in Sydney Harbour. Around the same time, Monty was voted "Beard of the Year" for 2006. It wasn't an award that he was expecting!

Disaster!

The Ashes tour turned out to be a disaster for England as they lost all five tests. This was the first time this had happened since 1920–21. By the end of it Monty was one of the few England players who had improved their reputation.

Monty said that he learned a lot from watching Shane Warne bowl during the first two Ashes matches.

Monty was asked to remain in Australia for the **one-day** series against Australia and New Zealand (see map on page 12). This was a surprise to him and he'd already been making plans for when he got home. However, he knew that if he did well he might be chosen to play in the cricket World Cup later in 2007.

Monty made his one-day international **debut** against Australia on 12 January 2007. England lost the match but Monty took the **wicket** of Matthew Hayden, a player Monty had met when he first started playing at Northamptonshire. England went on to win the series, which helped to cheer them up after the terrible **Ashes** defeat.

PRACTICE MAKES PERFECT

One of the main reasons why a sportsperson is able to reach the top of his or her field is because they work very hard. Monty is a good example of this. He often continues training and practising long after the other players have finished. He and Northamptonshire teammate, Mike Hussey, used to have their own battles in the **nets** after all the other players had gone home.

The Northamptonshire captain, David Sales, has said about Monty: "He's always trying to find out what people think. Most of all he's keen to know the batsman's point of view." It is this desire to learn that makes Monty a better player than many other cricketers.

In the nets, players can practise against a machine called Merlyn. Merlyn "bowls" balls at the person batting, in different ways to represent the different styles of bowling used in matches.

Wisden Cricketer of the Year

In March 2007, Monty was named as one of the five Wisden Cricketers of the Year. *The Wisden Almanack* is a book that comes out once a year and is filled with facts and figures about the cricketing world. Each year they list their five best players based mainly on the previous season in England. Players can only be named in the list once in their career. It is seen as a huge honour.

Monty was chosen to play for England at the World Cup but he struggled. He had a difficult game against South Africa, but did get 3 wickets for 25 **runs** against Bangladesh. Unfortunately, however, England failed to get through to the semi-finals.

The test series against the West Indies came quickly after the World Cup. Monty had a great series and took 23 **wickets**. In the Third test, he took 10 wickets for just 187 **runs**. Monty was voted "man of the match". He went on to become England's "player of the series".

Monty has never tried alcohol. When he won the bottle of champagne as his prize for being man of the match, he didn't drink it but saved the unopened bottle as a trophy.

Monty is very enthusiastic, as he shows nearly every time he gets a wicket. However, some people believe that he goes too far sometimes when appealing for wickets. It is the umpire who has to decide whether the person batting is out or not. Over-the-top appealing can be seen as putting pressure on the umpire to declare a player out. This goes against the spirit of **fair play** in cricket.

ICC RANKINGS

The ICC has a way of ranking (ordering) players throughout the world. There are lists for tests and **one-day** games, as well as separate rankings for batting and bowling. The players are marked on each international game they play, and their total points are compared to those of other players. The player with the most points at any one time is number one on the list.

Most cricketers do not think about rankings all the time. However, there is a sense of pride when any player manages to improve their position in the rankings. Monty reached number six in the test bowling rankings in June 2007. This was the highest position of his career so far and he was only 25!

A well-known Sikh

Monty is no longer just a cricketer. In June 2007, Monty was asked to join other important people for a celebration. It was to celebrate 60 years of **independence** from Britain for India and Pakistan. This was not a sporting celebration, but Monty was asked to join in because he is one of the best known **Sikhs** in Britain.

During the series against the West Indies, Monty played brilliantly. Here, he is about to bowl out Runako Morton in the first test match at Lord's.

India toured England in the second half of the 2007 season. It wasn't a great series for Monty and his best was 4 **wickets** for 101 **runs** in the second test. It wasn't a good series for England either as they lost 1–0. Unfortunately it became famous more for the behaviour of the players. The Indian batters were not happy when a jellybean sweet was found on the wicket, the area where the batters have to run. Monty was not **fielding** close to the area on the pitch where the jellybean was found but he thought that it must have happened accidentally.

The Sri Lankan tour

In October 2007, the England team travelled to Sir Lanka. Monty was not chosen to play in the first four **one-day** games – it was his old Northamptonshire rival, Graeme Swann, who was picked for his better batting ability. Monty was still picked for the test team, however, and was even called "(England's) number one Test spinner" by the England coach, Peter Moores. However, Monty ended up with only eight wickets from the series.

The New Zealand tour

Things looked up for Monty, however, when he played on the tour of New Zealand. The spinner managed his career best figures of 6 wickets for 126 runs in the final test in Napier. Monty is now edging closer to the first great milestone in an international bowler's career – 100 wickets! He's got 92 so far and hopefully he'll be able to reach 100 wickets over the summer of 2008 when New Zealand and South Africa visit England.

Cricket really can be played anywhere! Here, Monty and fellow England players, Owais Shah and Matt Prior, play cricket outside the Houses of Parliament in London.

A different Monty

In between the cricket matches, Monty has found time to have some fun. He had to dress up in a dark suit, bowler hat and carry an umbrella. This dressing up was for an advert for cricket sponsors Npower. This gave Monty's teammates plenty of opportunities to make fun of him!

English cricket has certainly been affected by the appearance of Monty Panesar in the international team. David Parsons, the ECB spin-bowling coach, said in 2006: "I'm so pleased people are talking about spin bowling again because it has been overlooked for so long. The Monty effect this year has been amazing and we need to make the most of that."

Monty's first cricket club, Luton Town and Indians, has seen many more children wanting to play for the team since Monty began to play for England. This situation has also been seen elsewhere around the country. As Monty has become more popular, he has started to take part in masterclasses (lessons) for children of different ages to help them learn the art of spin bowling. For children, meeting someone who is enthusiastic about the game helps them to develop faster.

Monty demonstrates spin bowling to another group of enthusiastic children.

Monty Panesar arrives at the UK premiere of Die Hard 4.0 in Leicester Square, London.

Life outside cricket

Monty has also become involved in some charity work in 2007. Charlotte Edwards, the England women's team captain, asked if he would play in a special **Twenty20** match she was arranging. The game was played between some of the women's team and a selection of the men's team, past and present, in order to raise money for Macmillan Nurses. Monty and Charlotte also helped launch NatWest CricketForce 2006, a campaign to help local clubs get ready for the new season.

Monty was **nominated** for the ICC Test Player of the Year after taking 42 **wickets** in the previous year. He didn't win but it was an honour to be in the running for the award.

His autobiography was published in 2007 and he has his own website. He is asked to events that just two years ago he would not even have been considered for. He actually went along to the first showing of the film *Die Hard 4.0* in London but unfortunately didn't get to meet his favourite actor, Bruce Willis!

Monty is now easily recognised by cricket fans and is even becoming known to those who know nothing about cricket. He has certainly come a long way in a short time.

25 April 1982	Monty is born in Luton, Bedfordshire.
25 April 1992	Monty is given his first cricket bat as a birthday present.
1998	Monty is awarded a sports **scholarship** to Bedford Modern School.
23 August 2001	Monty's first-class **debut** for Northamptonshire against Leicestershire.
2001	Monty wins the Denis Compton award.
2001	Monty begins a university degree at Loughborough University
August 2002	Monty's first **one-day** game against Essex.
January 2006	Monty's international test debut against India.
June 2006	Monty's first international test five-wicket haul ("five-for") against Sri Lanka.
12 Jan 2007	Monty's international one-day debut against Australia.
March 2007	Monty is named as one of the five Wisden Cricketers of the Year.
11 June 2007	Monty's first international test "ten-for" against West Indies.
11 June 2007	Monty's first "Man of the match" award.
11 June 2007	Monty's first "Man of the series" award.
June 2007	Monty reaches the highest position in the ICC rankings.
August 2007	Monty is **nominated** for the ICC Test Player of the Year award.

- Monty loves music, including R&B and Bhangra. Bhangra music is "a sort of Punjabi hip-hop" according to Monty.

- Monty does not like dogs.

- Monty once scored a century (100 **runs**, a big milestone for when batting) while playing for Dunstable Town.

- There were 35 members of Monty's family at the test against India in Mohali, India, in March 2006.

- Monty has his own newspaper column in the *Daily Mail*.

- Monty is the ninth player to be chosen to play cricket for England whose family originally comes from India.

- At Lord's, in the match against India in 2007, Monty got to meet *Harry Potter* star, Daniel Radcliffe. Daniel was spending his 18th birthday watching the match.

- Monty is also a keen football fan. He supports his local team, Luton Town and loves watching Arsenal play.

- When he was at school Monty played on the school football team. He plays as a striker or midfielder whenever he and his friends have five-a-side matches.

- In 2007 Monty did an advert for a new flavour of Walkers crisps – chilli and lemon.

Ashes series of five tests played between England and Australia every two years

debut first appearance of a player

facilities equipment and space available for a certain activity

fair play sporting behaviour, which means not deliberately putting other players off their game

fast bowler someone who bowls at around 129–145 kph (80–90 mph)

fees money that has to be paid to attend a school

fielding taking catches, chasing after the ball, and throwing to save as many runs as possible while the opposition is batting

first-class county cricket professional cricket at county level

independence freedom from the control of other people or countries

innings either the length of time that one player bats for or the length of time that the whole team bats for. The innings is over when the tenth batter is out. This is because there must always be two players batting at one time. The innings can also be over when the batting team declare.

medium pace bowler someone who bowls at around 113–129 kph (70–80 mph)

nets area surrounded by netting and used by players for cricket practice

nominate put forward for an award

one-day match type of cricket match where each innings lasts for either 40 or 50 overs

over an over consists of six balls in a row bowled by the same bowler

patka type of headgear worn by some Sikhs

role model successful person whose behaviour is imitated by others

run a run is given to the batting team when the two batters have run from one end of the wicket to another

scholarship when a student's school fees are paid for by the school itself

Sikh someone who follows the Indian religion of Sikhism

spin bowler someone who bowls at around 88–105 kph (55–65 mph). The slower pace means that spinners have to bowl lots of variations.

test match game of cricket that can last up to five days with each team playing two innings

Twenty20 type of cricket where each innings lasts for only 20 overs

wicket another word for the pitch, or the three stumps (posts) at each end of the pitch. A person who is batting is said to have lost his or her wicket when they are given out.

Useful addresses

England and Wales Cricket Board (ECB)
Lord's Cricket Ground
London NW8 8QZ
Tel: 020 7432 1200
www.ecb.co.uk

The International Cricket Council (ICC)
P.O.Box 500070
Dubai
United Arab Emirates
www.icc-cricket.com

Books

Know the Game: Cricket, Marylebone Cricket Club (A & C Black, 2004)

The Making of a Champion: A World-class Cricketer, Andrew Langley (Heinemann Library, 2005)

Monty's Turn: My Story So Far, Monty Panesar (Hodder & Stoughton, 2007)

The Ultimate Guide to Cricket, Gavin Mortimer (Puffin Books, 2006)

Websites

http://www.cricinfo.com
This site gives reports of current and historical matches.

http://news.bbc.co.uk/sport
You can access scorecards from the current season's matches that Monty has played
in from this site.

http://www.monty-panesar.com
Monty's own website has all the latest news about his career.

Disclaimer

All the Internet addresses (URLs) given in this book were valid at the time of going to press. However, due to the dynamic nature of the Internet, some addresses may have changed, or sites may have changed or ceased to exist since publication. While the author and Publishers regret any inconvenience this may cause readers, no responsibility for any such changes can be accepted by either the author or the Publishers. It is recommended that adults supervise children on the Internet.

Ashes tour 17, 18-19
Atherton, Mike 15
Australia 5, 17, 18, 20
Australian National Academy
    11, 12

Bangladesh 21
British Universities team 9
Brown, Jason 10

children and sport 26
coaching 7, 11

Edwards, Charlotte 27
England 10, 12-13, 14, 16,
    18-19, 20, 21, 22, 23, 24
England and Wales Cricket
    Board (ECB) 12, 17

fair play 22, 24
fast bowlers 5
first-class county cricket 10
Flintoff, Andrew 19

Giles, Ashley 12, 16, 18

Hayden, Matthew 20
Hussey, Mike 20

India (country) 6, 23
India (cricket team) 12-13, 24
innings 12, 14
International Cricket Council
    (ICC) Champions Trophy 17
International Cricket Council
    (ICC) test rankings 4, 22

Khan, Younis 16

Leicestershire 10
Loughborough Cricket Centre of
    Excellence 9
Luton Town and Indians Cricket
    Club 7, 26

Marsh, Rod 11
medium pace bowlers 8
Merlin machine 21
Moores, Peter 24
Morton, Runako 23
Muralitharan, Muttiah 5, 14

New Zealand 4
Northamptonshire 4, 5, 9, 10,
    11, 15, 20

one-day series 4, 20, 24
over-the-top appealing 22

Pakistan 16
Panesar, Monty
    amazing facts 29
    autobiography 27
    batting and bowling style 4, 8
    celebrity status 5, 16, 23, 27
    charity work 27
    childhood 6-7
    Denis Compton award 10
    education 8, 9
    England player 10, 12-13,
        14, 16, 18-19, 20, 21, 22,
        23, 24
    family 4, 6, 29
    fielding 11, 12, 13, 15, 16, 24
    galloping celebrations 5, 12
    ICC test ranking 4, 22
    Northamptonshire player 4,
        5, 10, 11, 15, 20
    Wisden Cricketer of the Year
        21
Parsons, David 26
patka 14, 16
Prior, Matt 25

role models 14
rules of cricket 8

Sales, David 20
Shah, Owais 25

Sikhism 6, 14, 23
sledging 24
South Africa 21
spin bowlers 5, 8, 14, 26
Sri Lanka 5, 9, 10, 14, 24
Swann, Graeme 10, 11, 24

Tendulkar, Sachin 12, 13
test matches 12-13, 14, 16, 18,
    22, 23, 24
training 20, 21
Twenty20 competition 5, 15, 27

Warne, Shane 5, 19
Wessels, Kepler 11
West Indies 22, 23
wicket milestones 14
Wisden Cricketer of the Year 21
women's cricket 27
World Cup 20, 21